Living in

CAMBRIDGE
UNIVERSITY PRESS

A Caribbean island

St Lucia is a small island in the Caribbean Sea. It is hot all year round and it often rains. The rain is very heavy but it soon dries in the bright sunshine. There are mountains on the island. They were made by volcanoes. It is a very green and beautiful place. Bananas grow there and parrots live in the dense rainforest. It is not surprising that people like living in St Lucia and that many tourists go there on holiday.

In some ways St Lucia is changing. In this book you will find out more about the island, the people who live there and how it is changing. When you have found out about these things you will be able to answer these questions:

What is it like to live in St Lucia?

How does it compare with the place where you live?

Things to find

Look at the map of St Lucia.

- Which two places would you most like to visit? Why?
- Which things grow well in St Lucia?

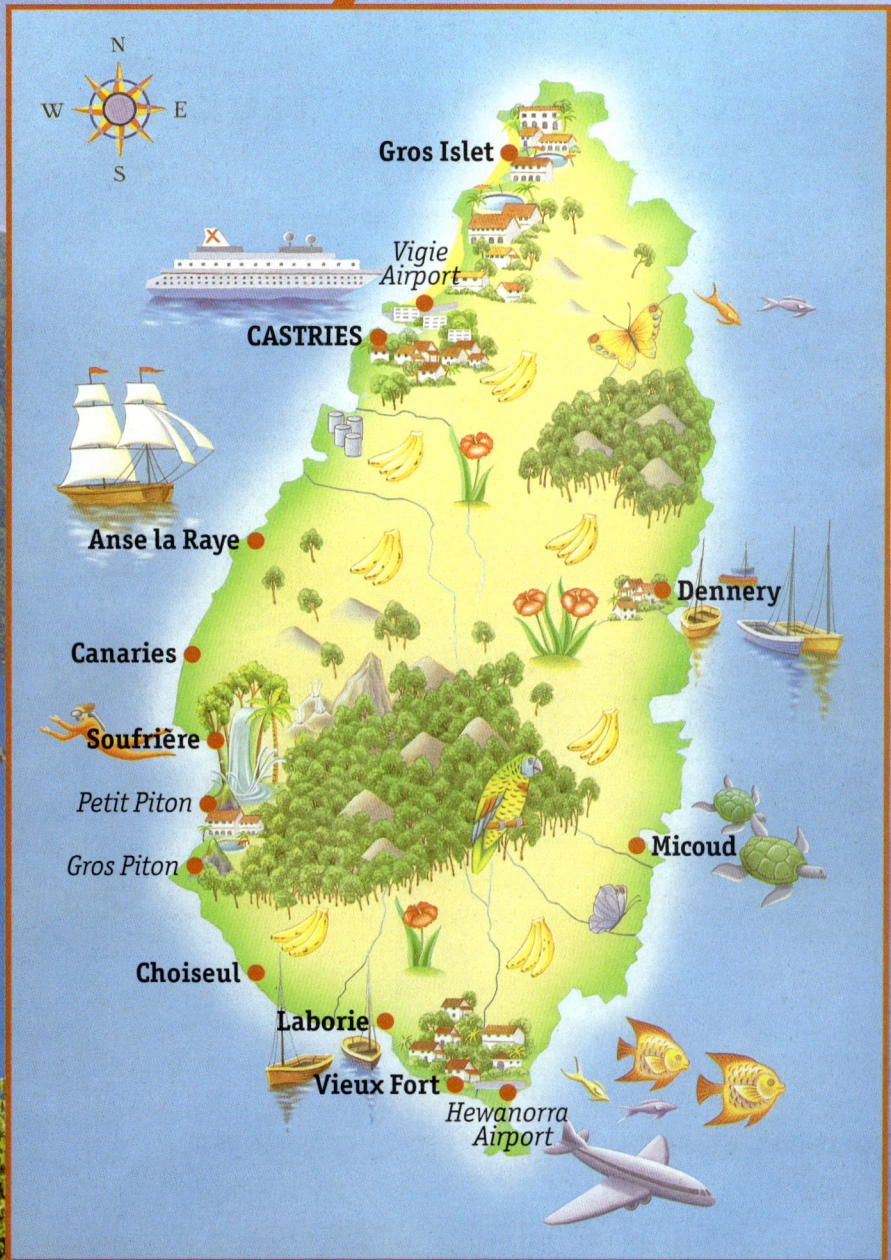

Gros Islet

Vigie Airport

CASTRIES

Anse la Raye

Canaries

Soufrière

Petit Piton

Gros Piton

Dennery

Micoud

Choiseul

Laborie

Vieux Fort

Hewanorra Airport

N
W E
S

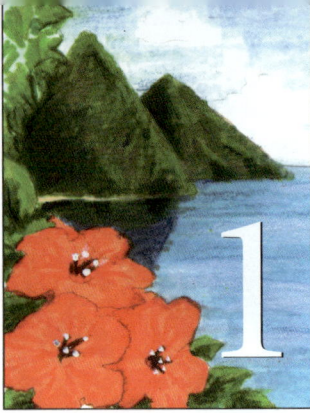

The Harvey family

Mr and Mrs Harvey and their four children live at Mon Giraud near Castries, which is the only city in St Lucia. Here are some pictures of them and their home. They are going to tell you about living in St Lucia.

What is life like for the Harvey family?

Mr Harvey says: *'We live in a modern bungalow on a steep hillside. One side of our house stands on stilts. My workshop is underneath the verandah. I keep St Lucians cool by fixing their air conditioning and fridges.'*

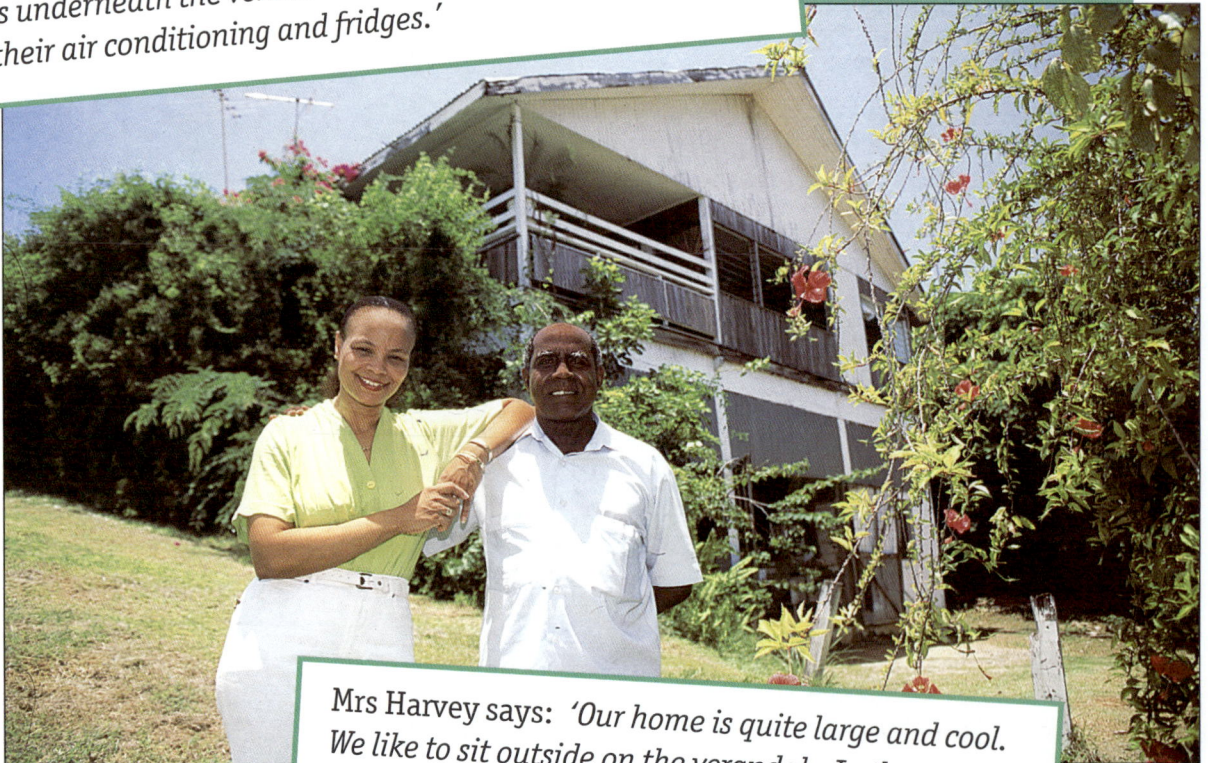

Mrs Harvey says: *'Our home is quite large and cool. We like to sit outside on the verandah. In the garden there are 15 different kinds of tropical fruit, such as mangoes and sugar apples. Ours was one of the first houses built. Now we have lots of neighbours.'*

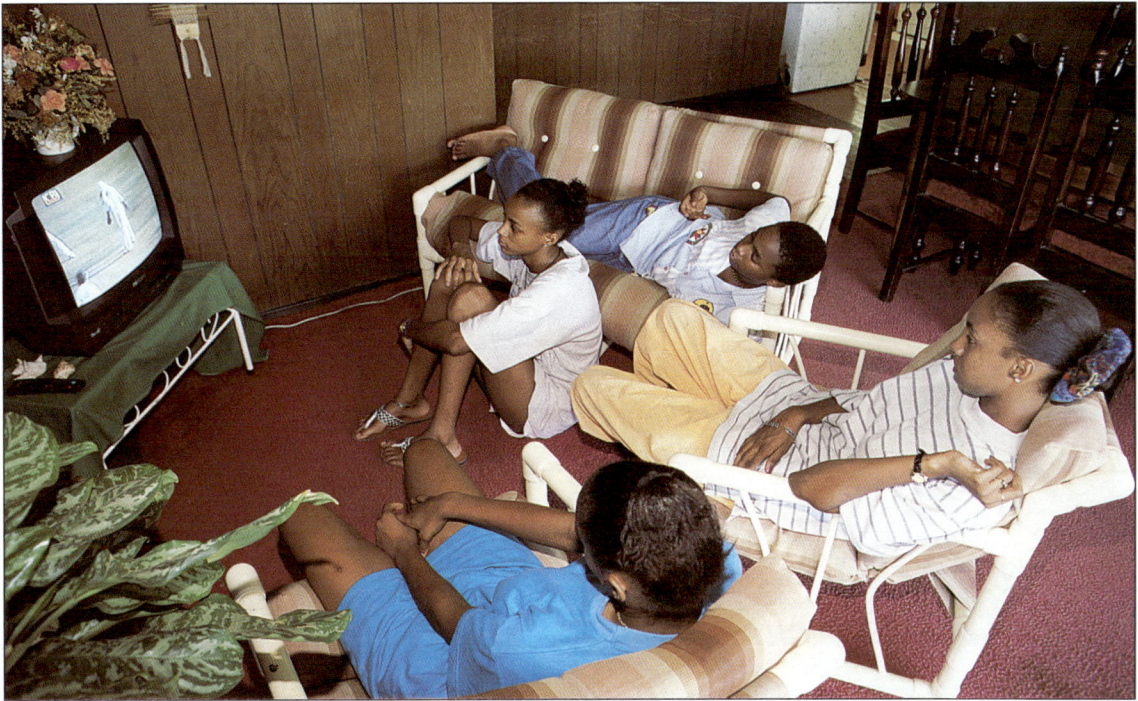

There are four children in the Harvey family. The youngest child is a boy called Gimel. He has three older sisters: Thia, Evvery and Hayle.

In the kitchen, the Harveys have two fridges for food and drinks. They store water in containers because the water supply is often turned off. It is very hot so the children usually wear shorts and T-shirts at home. They do not need shoes in the house or have covers on their beds.

Hayle says: 'We have a lovely view from our verandah. It looks out over Mount Pimard and the Rodney Bay Marina. We used to live at Vigie with a view over Castries harbour. We could watch all the boats coming and going.'

Think about

- Why do you think the Harveys spend a lot of time outside?

- Why is Mr Harvey's work so important in St Lucia?

- Is the Harvey's home like yours? In what ways is it different?

Where the Harveys live

Gimel

'This is my map of where we live at Mon Giraud. You come along the Gros Islet Highway from Castries and turn up to the left near Sunny Villas. There are three tracks. You take the middle one and turn right when it divides. The track is very rough and full of potholes.'

Thia

'Our house is on the left. It is surrounded by trees and bushes. We play cricket in the garden. Our dog will bark at you when you arrive, but he is quite friendly.'

Evvery

'We have cats and kittens too. They are my special favourites. The house is built of wood, called greenheart. It has a steel roof.'

Mr. David and family

Ms. Vidy

← to Castries

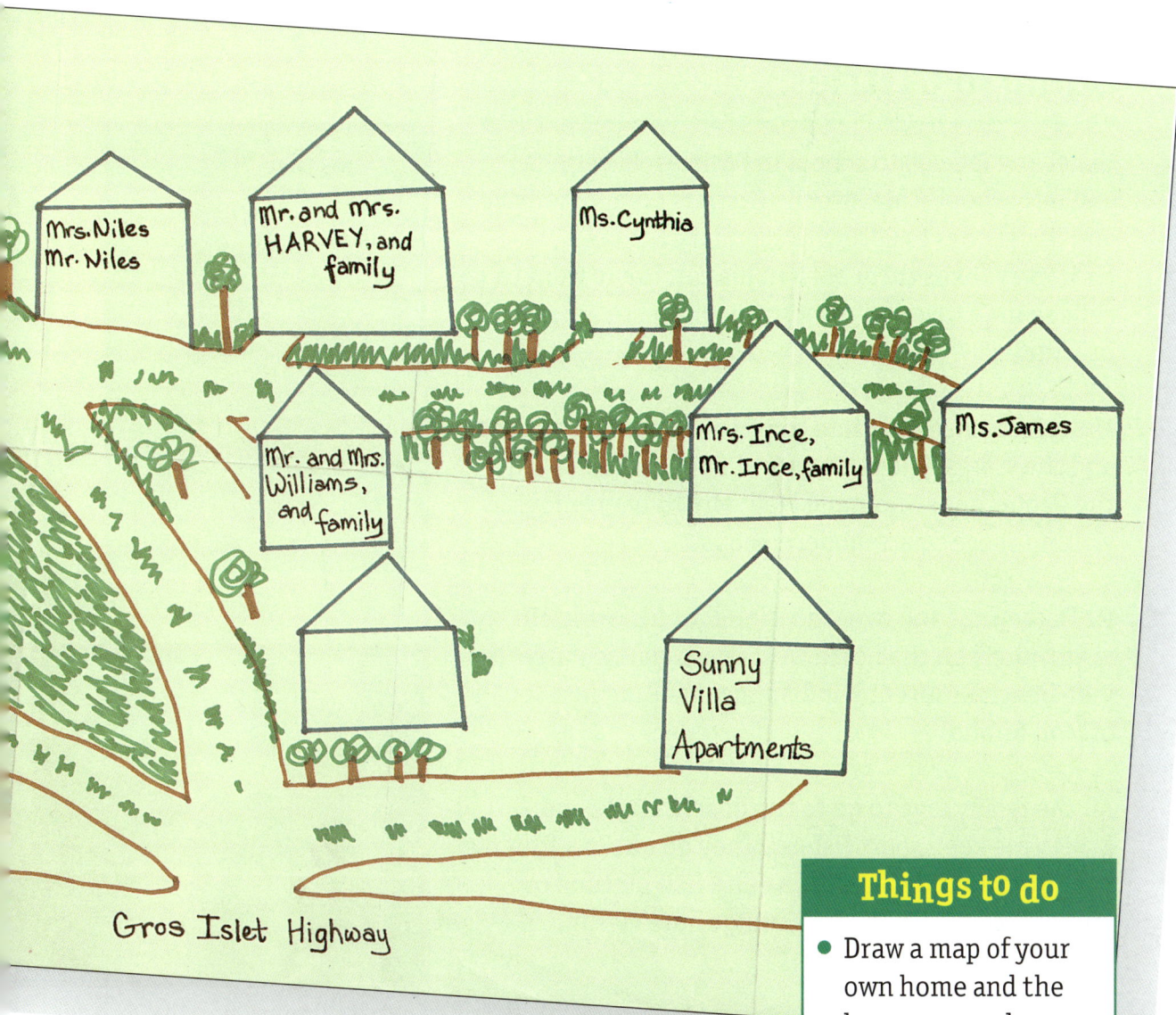

Mrs. Niles
Mr. Niles

Mr. and Mrs.
HARVEY, and
family

Ms. Cynthia

Mr. and Mrs.
Williams,
and family

Mrs. Ince,
Mr. Ince, family

Ms. James

Sunny
Villa
Apartments

Gros Islet Highway

Things to do

- Draw a map of your own home and the homes around you.

- Write down the directions to your home as Gimel has done.

This picture was taken from the air. The pointer shows you which is the Harvey's house.

Going to Castries

Gimel and Thia go to school in Castries; Evvery has just left school. Thia attends Castries Comprehensive and Gimel goes to Corinth Secondary School. Mr Harvey takes them both in his car. Hayle went to college in Castries but is now finishing her studies in Trinidad.

Mrs Harvey also goes into town to shop in the market and the stores. There is a new shopping area called the Gablewoods Shopping Mall. Mrs Harvey enjoys visiting these smart modern shops.

Mr Harvey goes all over the island for his work. He visits hotels on the north west coast, particularly the Villa Beach Resort at Windjammer Landing just south of Mon Giraud.

All the family love to go to the beach. Hayle and Evvery are keen sport fishers. They go out in a friend's boat from Rodney Bay Marina and fish for tuna or billfish. They long to catch a huge blue marlin.

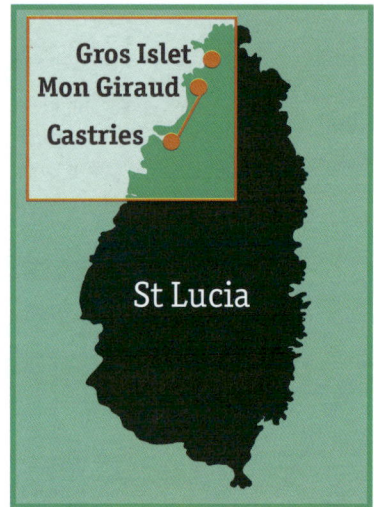

St Lucia

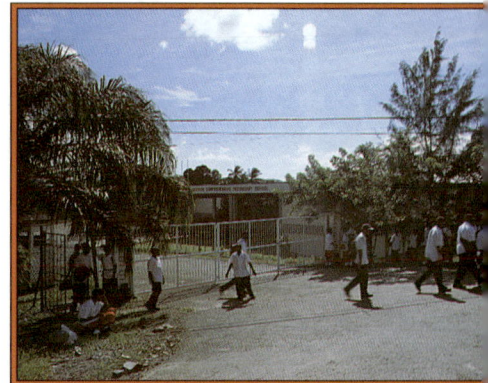

Castries Comprehensive School.

Things to do

- List the main features which the Harveys pass as they drive home from Castries.

- Make a map of your journey to school. Show some of the important places you pass on the way.

Vigie Airport.

Villa Beach Resort, Windjammer Landing.

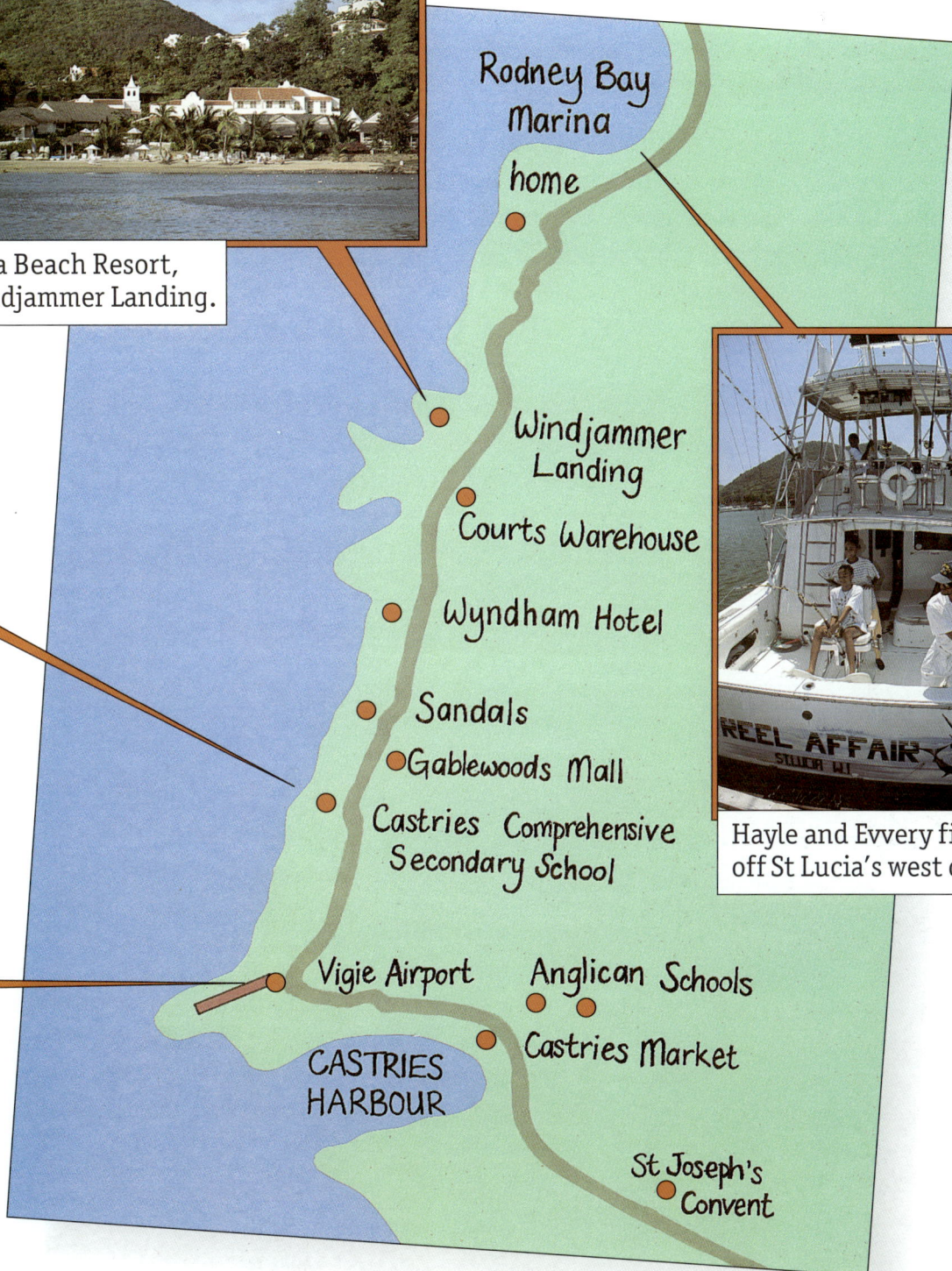

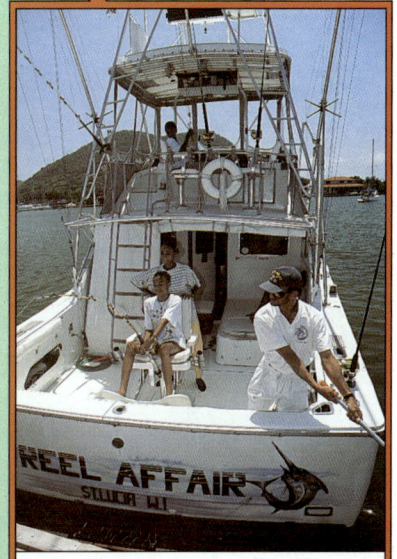

The Harvey family have to travel nearly every day. Thia has drawn a map to show you where they go.

Rodney Bay Marina
home

Windjammer Landing

Courts Warehouse

Wyndham Hotel

Sandals

Gablewoods Mall

Castries Comprehensive Secondary School

Vigie Airport   Anglican Schools

CASTRIES HARBOUR   Castries Market

St Joseph's Convent

Hayle and Evvery fishing off St Lucia's west coast.

9

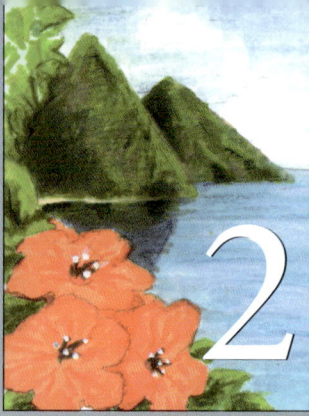

St Lucia – a special place

St Lucia is very hot and wet. There are many mountains on the island. They were made by volcanoes. Much of the island is covered in subtropical forest. People have come from many different places to live in St Lucia – including America, Europe, Africa and Asia.

What makes St Lucia special?

Many pictures of St Lucia show the Pitons. You can see them in the photograph on this page. They are steep-sided peaks which rise straight out of the sea near Soufrière. They were formed by volcanoes. There are not many flat places on St Lucia. Most of them are on the coast where the rivers run into the sea. This is where most of the villages have grown up.

Hardwood trees such as greenheart and mahogany grow in the forest. Creepers, ferns and dense undergrowth make walking difficult. Some plants grow on the branches of the trees. Many animals such as the boa constrictor snake and Jacquot, the rare St Lucian parrot, live in the forest.

It is very hot and sunny all year round. East winds from the Atlantic Ocean help to keep the people cool. The rain falls very heavily over the high mountains but on the coasts it can be very dry and cactus plants grow in some places.

▲ Tall trees, creepers, ferns and rare flowers such as the St Lucian orchid grow in the rainforest. ▼

▲ Jacquot, the St Lucian parrot, and snakes such as boa constrictors live in the trees. ▶

Think about

Think about the weather and the landscape in St Lucia.

- What do you like about the island?

- Do you think there might be any problems? Explain them.

Tropical storms

There can be storms and hurricanes in the Caribbean from July to November. They can damage homes and crops and sometimes people are injured or even killed.

In the early hours of 10 September 1994, St Lucia was hit by a fierce tropical storm. Storms like these are given names. This one was called 'Debbie'. It did a great deal of damage. Most of it was caused by the very heavy rain which filled rivers with rocks and stones, causing floods and landslides all over the island. High winds added to the damage.

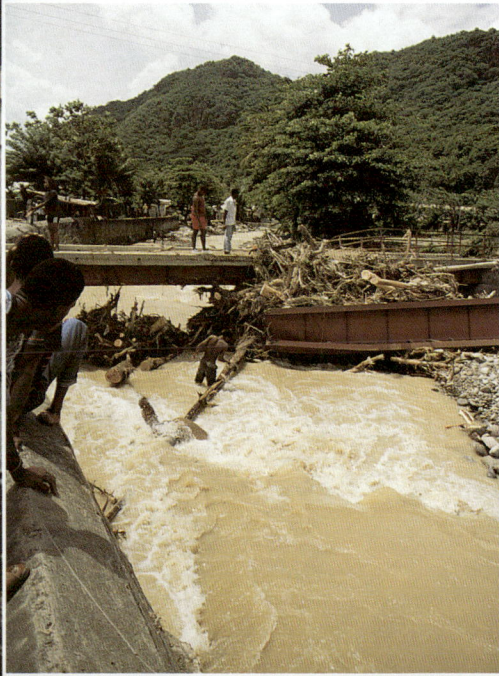

Villages on the coast were flooded and four people died. The school in Soufrière was half buried in mud. Crops were flattened. An important road and several bridges were swept away.

Damage to Soufrière after tropical storm Debbie.

DEBBIE DOES DAMAGE

2 dead, more than 35 homeless

Leonita Esnard's home was nearly swept out to sea with herself and her two children inside it. Fortunately the house was trapped behind coconut trees which saved their lives.

Sylvia Lawrenson was up to her neck in water inside her house. Her crippled husband was rescued by young villagers.

The Prime Minister said: 'Half the banana crop was destroyed, more than half the coconut harvest lost, and thousands of animals were drowned.'

St Lucia will take many years to recover. One eye-witness said: 'I went to the school, to where the typing room used to be. The room was gone. Only one typewriter was left on the ground. In the library there were only about five books. The whole place was covered in sand and mud.'

Things to do

- Make a picture story of what happened during tropical storm Debbie. These are some of the things you could draw:

  the storm washing rocks down rivers

  houses damaged by mud

  banana trees falling over

  a school badly damaged by floods and winds

These children have made a display in their school about the history of the St Lucian people.

One of the things which makes St Lucia special is the mixture of people who live here.

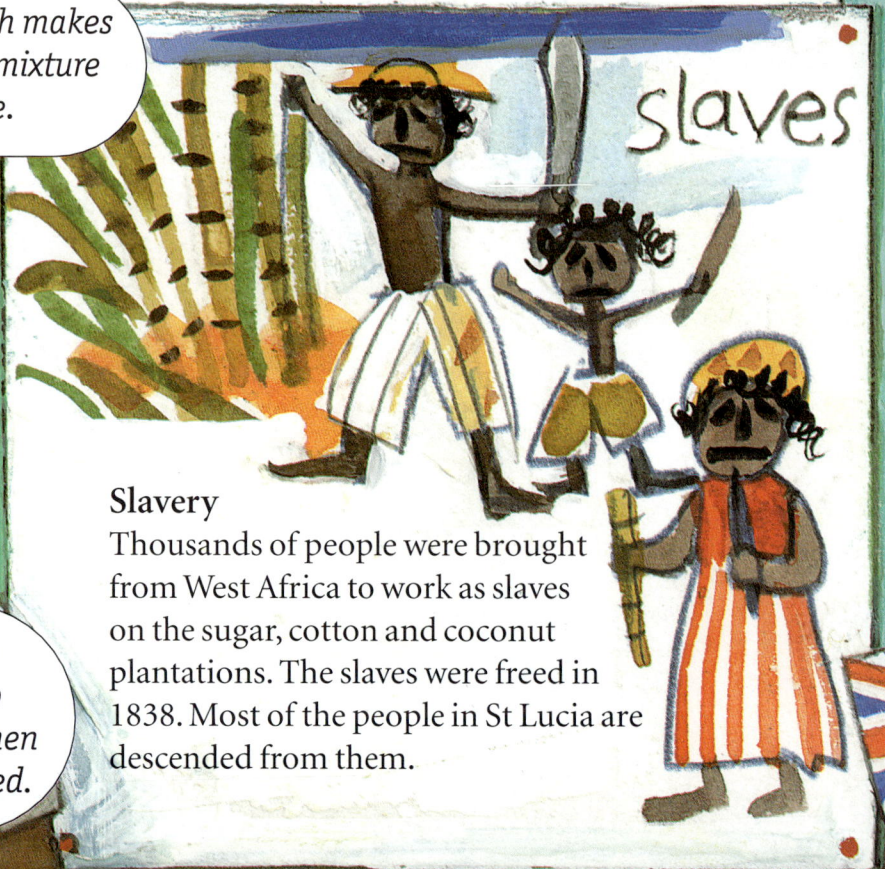

Many other people came from India to work in St Lucia when the slaves were freed.

St Lucian people

Arawaks and Caribs

The first people to settle in St Lucia were South American Indians called Arawaks and Caribs. They lived by fishing and farming. Pieces of pottery, human remains and rock carvings help us to learn about the island's early history. The Caribs fought with the Arawaks and made them leave St Lucia. About 140,000 people from different races live in St Lucia today.

The Arawaks used to live in homes like this. ▶

slaves

Slavery

Thousands of people were brought from West Africa to work as slaves on the sugar, cotton and coconut plantations. The slaves were freed in 1838. Most of the people in St Lucia are descended from them.

RAWAK

In the 17th and 18th centuries, the French and the English fought each other for control of St Lucia. English is still the official language but many St Lucians speak 'patois' – a language based on French. Songs, dances and street names all show how important the French language still is.

This is my picture of an Arawak rock carving. It shows a father, a mother and a child.

Things to do

● Different people had different reasons for going to St Lucia. How many reasons can you think of?

Places to live

Nearly half of the people in St Lucia live in the capital city, Castries. It is by far the biggest town on the island. Castries is also a port. It has the most sheltered harbour in the Caribbean. Big ships can dock there. They carry people and goods, especially the bananas which St Lucians sell overseas.

The biggest towns and villages are all at the mouths of rivers around the coast. They are linked by a single main road. There are also small roads linking the banana plantations to the main road.

▶ This map shows the main towns and villages in St Lucia. It also shows the main road.

Think about

- Where are the biggest towns, villages and the main road? Why do you think they are there?

- What is special about the place names in St Lucia?

0   10 km

⬤	capital city
◼	town
⬤	village
～	main road
🟩	very high ground

Gros Islet

Anse la Raye

Dennery

Canaries

Soufrière

Micoud

Choiseul

Laborie

Vieux Fort

▲ This is Castries.
Find it on the map. In the photograph you can see the government buildings and some fishing boats.

● Why do you think Castries grew there?

▲ This is Vieux Fort.
Find it on the map.
What type of place
is this?

▲ This is Anse la Raye.
Find it on the map.
What sort of place is it?
Is it bigger or smaller
than Castries?

Things to do

● Imagine you work for a holiday company. Write and draw a booklet to tell people all the special things about St Lucia. You could mention the scenery, the wildlife and plants, the weather, the history and the people.

● If you were the Prime Minister are there any changes you would make? Think about houses, schools, roads and problems with storms.

Castries – the capital city

Castries is the most important town and port in St Lucia. Many St Lucians live or work there. Others go to school in Castries or do their shopping there.

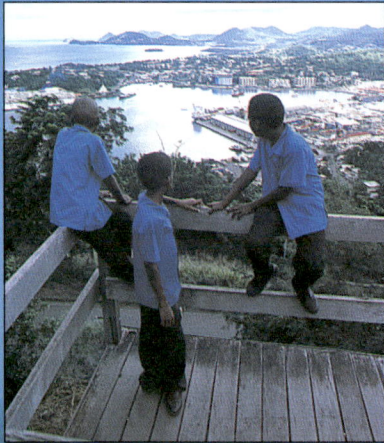

What is in Castries?

◀ These St Lucian children have a new boy in their class at school. He is staying in St Lucia for a few months. Today they are standing on the top of Morne Fortune, a high hill just outside Castries. From there the children can point out many places to see in Castries.

Look at this picture of Castries. ▶
- Describe what you can see.

Things to find

Look at this list of places in Castries. How many of them can you find in the picture?

A container ship taking bananas to England

Cranes in the docks to lift the huge containers

The tall white government buildings along the waterfront

The shops and offices in Castries

The houses in the hills around Castries where people live

● How many ships or boats can you see?

At school in Castries

Saria Torrance is 8 years old. She goes to the Anglican Primary School in Castries. This what she said about her school:

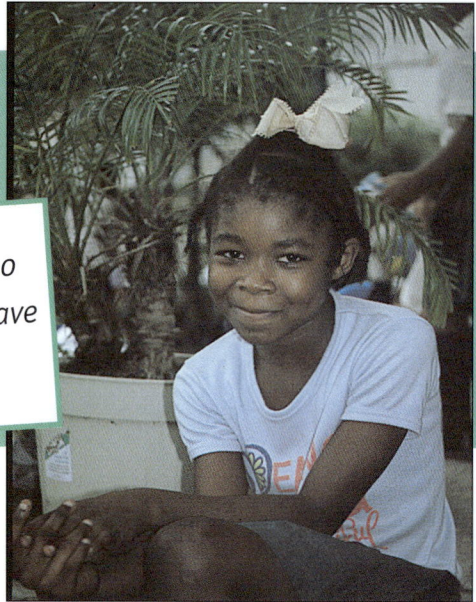

'It is a long way from my home in Dennery so I travel on a minibus called a transport. I have to pay a dollar for my fare each way.'

'I like my school. It is very big. There are 37 children in my class. We do English and mathematics, social studies and science. Sometimes we sing songs, play games and make pictures and models. We learn about St Lucia and Castries, our capital city. I like it when we go to the park to do PE and play ball games.'

'At break time we go in the school yard, playing chasing and singing games. I bring a sandwich for my lunch or I buy crisps and fruit from the tuck shop. After school I like to buy icicles or a lolly pop from Miss Molly at the school gate.'

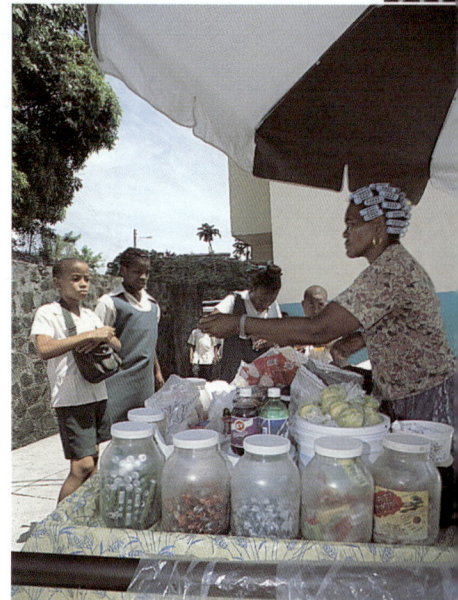

Things to do

- Describe the uniform worn at Saria's school.

- What is your school like? Draw and label some pictures of your school to show the children in St Lucia the things that are the same as their school and things that are different.

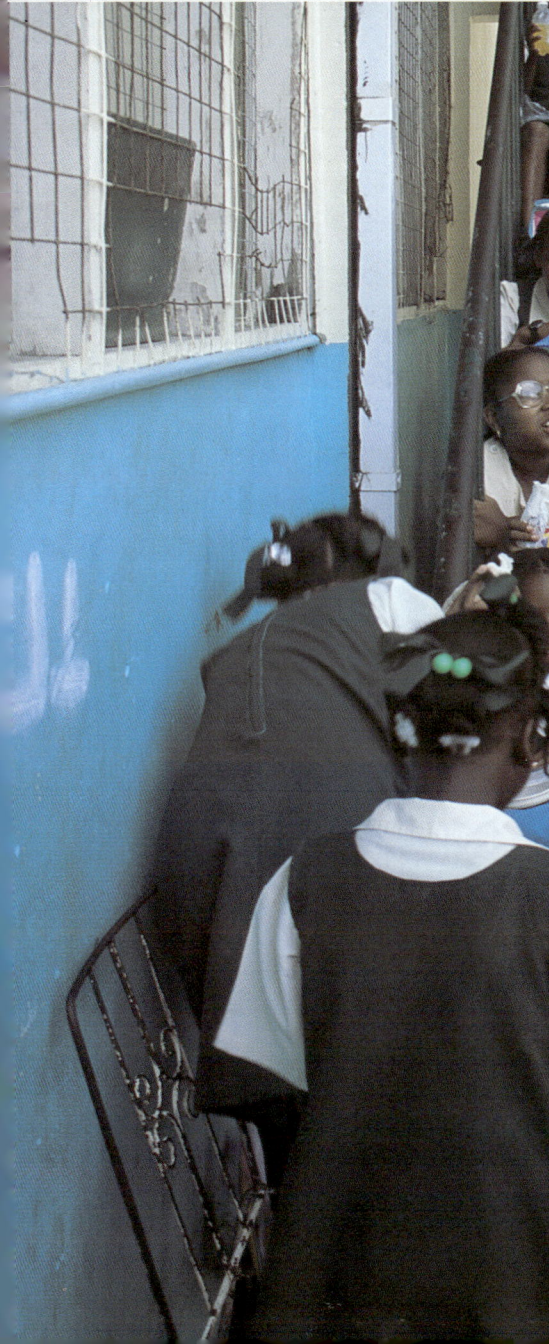

Going shopping

The Harvey children like going shopping to spend their pocket money. Gimel often buys sweets and drinks in a mini-market near home.

Fresh fruit and vegetables grow so widely over the island that farmers often sell them by the side of the road. Crowds gather around trucks piled high with coconuts – St Lucians love to drink the sweet coconut water.

▶ St Lucians buying coconuts.

◀ Gimel buying sweets from the mini-market.

Most of the family shopping is done in Castries. There are a few big shops which sell all sorts of things. Some shops are different to those in your high street but you might recognise others. There are also stalls on the pavement where you can buy hats, T-shirts and sweets.

● What do St Lucians buy here? ▶

◀ Mrs Harvey shopping at Gablewoods Mall.

Mrs Harvey says: 'Gablewoods Mall is a new shopping area. It is very smart and modern. I like to shop in the supermarket and visit the bookshop.'

This is the market in Castries. It is very large and colourful, with many exotic fruits and vegetables such as mangoes, pawpaws, sweet potatoes and breadfruit.

Think about

- Can you name any of the fruits and vegetables in the photograph?

- Is there a market like this near where you live?

▶ There is also a fish market where the local fishermen sell their catch.

◀ Tourists like to visit the markets but they also go to the shops which sell holiday items and souvenirs.

Things to do

- Copy these pictures and write the name of the place where you can buy the items shown in St Lucia.

- Do you like shopping? Where would you like to go shopping in St Lucia?

- Are the shops and markets in St Lucia like the ones where you live?

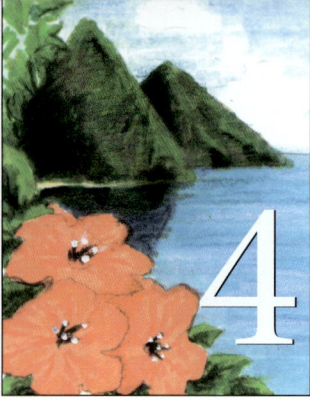

Places to go

The Harveys are soon going to have some visitors from England. Gimel and Thia are planning a really great day out for them. They each have different ideas about the best places to visit.

Where do St Lucians go for a day out?

▼ Gimel and Thia are deciding where to take their visitors.

Gimel wants to take the visitors for a cruise down the west coast on a sailing boat called the *Brig Unicorn*. Starting from Castries harbour the boat sails past villages, beaches and headlands on the way to Soufrière.

Gimel says: *'In the harbour we might see one of the enormous liners which take people on cruises around the Caribbean. Then we will sail past the big tanks of the oil terminal and the fishing boats at Anse la Raye. After we sail past Canaries, the Pitons will look really beautiful rising out of the sparkling sea. When the 'Brig Unicorn' gets to Soufrière the fishermen will come out on their surfboards to see if we want to buy any conch shells.'*

Things to do

- Where would you take visitors on a trip in your local area?
- Make a map to show the route.

Diamond Falls

Castries

oil terminal

Marigot Bay

Anse la Raye

Canaries

Soufrière

Diamond Falls

Pitons

Sulphur Springs

Sulphur Springs

'We could go to the "drive in volcano" at Sulphur Springs. Visitors are always amazed by the craters, steam, bubbling gas and the strong smell of bad eggs which sulphur makes. Not many people have seen an active volcano before! We could also visit the beautiful gardens and waterfall at Diamond Falls. After a swim, the 'Brig Unicorn' will take us back to Castries.'

Wonderful wildlife

Thia suggests taking the visitors over the mountains to the nature reserves on the east coast. To get there they would drive through the tall trees and brightly coloured flowers of the rainforest. This is the wettest place on the island. St Lucian parrots nest in the trees and boa constrictors curl up in the high branches. After going to the nature reserve they could collect sea moss at Savannes Bay on the coast. St Lucians use sea moss to make jelly which they eat with banana or mango.

Because it is so dry on the east coast, there are tall cactus plants which have red flowers and the trees are bent by the winds.

In the nature reserve on the Maria Islands at the southern end of St Lucia there are lizards and snakes, beautiful flowers and many different seabirds who nest there because it is so wild and peaceful.

▲ Lizards live in the Maria Islands Nature Reserve.

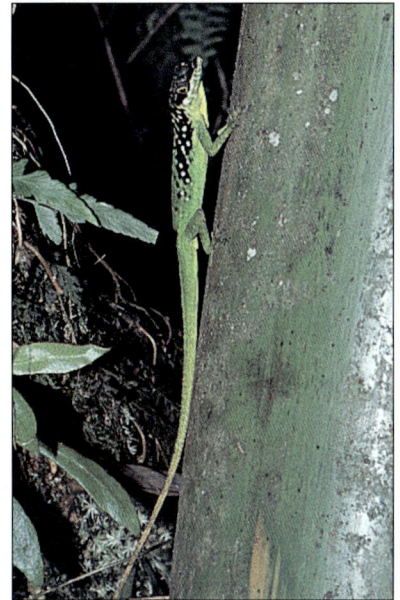

▲ The Maria Islands Nature Reserve.

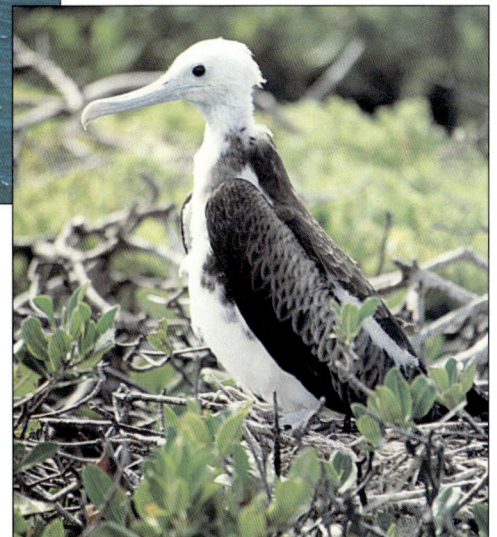

Things to do

- Imagine you are one of the visitors. Would you prefer to go with Gimel or Thia?

- Send a postcard home describing all the things you saw and heard on your day out.

- Draw the picture side of the postcard too. Some postcards have more than one picture.

▲ The black frigate bird is very rare. It only nests on Fregate Island.

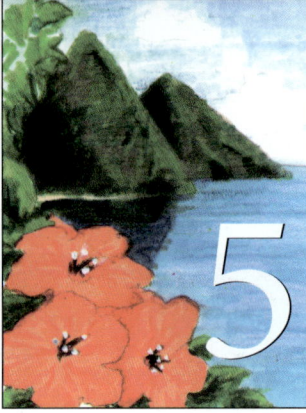

Working in St Lucia

There are many different jobs in St Lucia: growing bananas, fishing, making things in factories, cooking for tourists in hotels and many more. People have been doing some of these jobs – such as fishing and farming – for thousands of years. Some jobs, like those to do with holidays, are quite new.

How do people earn a living?

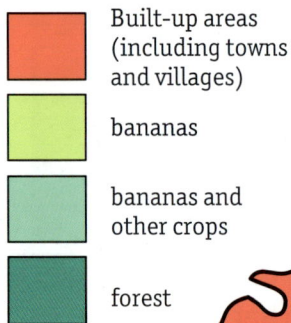

- Built-up areas (including towns and villages)
- bananas
- bananas and other crops
- forest

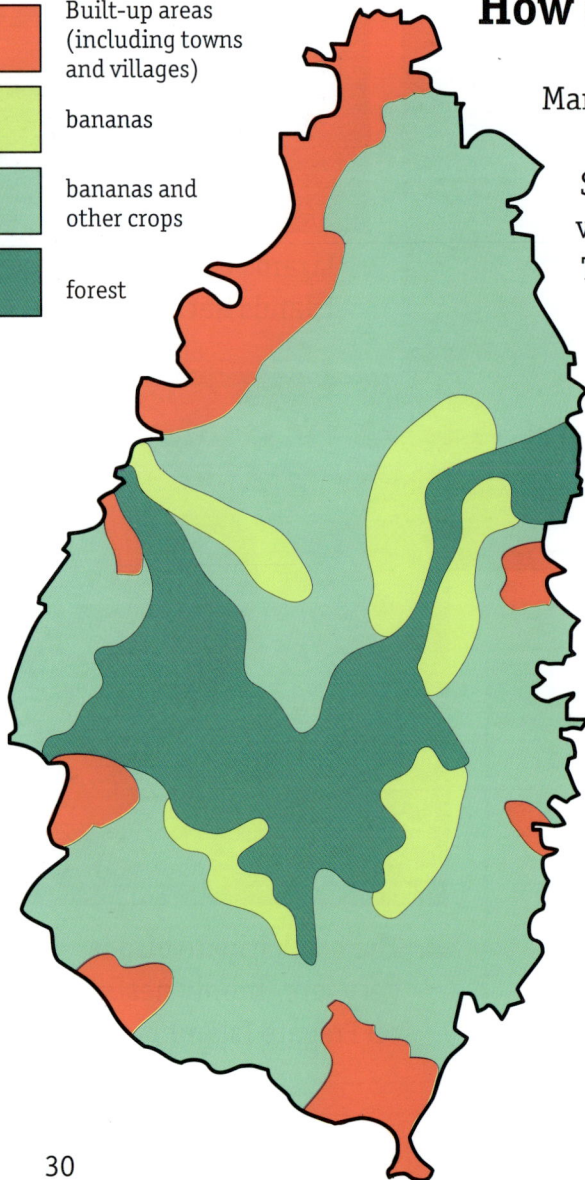

Many people in St Lucia work in farming. A hot, wet climate and fertile soils make St Lucia a good place to grow fruit and vegetables, especially on the flatter land. The crops grow well all year round. Bananas are the main crop but pineapples, coconuts and other tropical fruits are also grown.

◄ This map shows how land is used in St Lucia.

Think about

- Where are most of the built up areas?

- How much of the land is covered by forest?

- Why is St Lucia such a good place for growing things?

0   10
km

The Arawaks and Caribs came to St Lucia from South America in dug-out canoes. Each canoe is made from the trunk of a single tree. Some fishermen still make their fishing boats in this way but others prefer modern fibreglass boats. They last longer but they cost more to buy.

▶ You can see both kinds of boat in this picture.
  ● How is the dug-out canoe being made?

◀ Fish is an important food in St Lucia. The fish, like this huge swordfish, are probably different from those you eat.

Things to do

● People in St Lucia have been doing some jobs for many years. Draw and label some pictures of the things they produce.

Growing bananas

If you eat bananas, you have probably enjoyed one which was grown in St Lucia. For many years, bananas have been the most important thing grown or made in St Lucia. From the farmers who grow them, to the traders who sell them, half the families in St Lucia depend on bananas to make a living.

◄ You can often see bananas from St Lucia on sale in supermarkets in Britain.

These pictures show you how bananas are produced for you to eat.

1 Cutting bananas

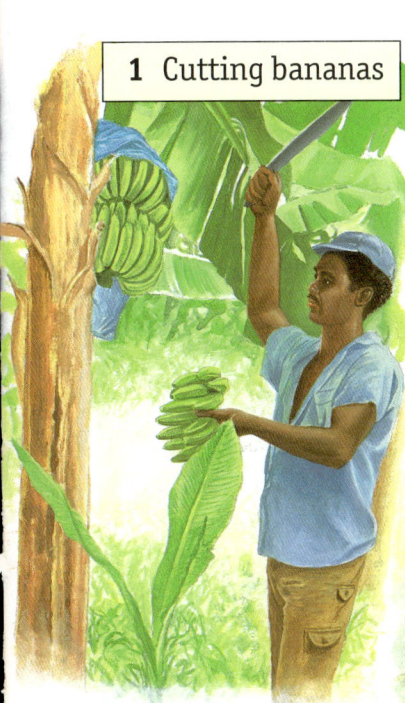

2 Drying bananas

3 Washing and packing

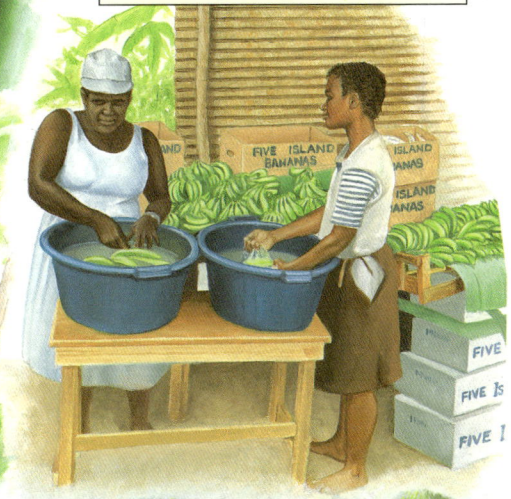

4 Taking bananas to the docks

5 Loading bananas on a ship

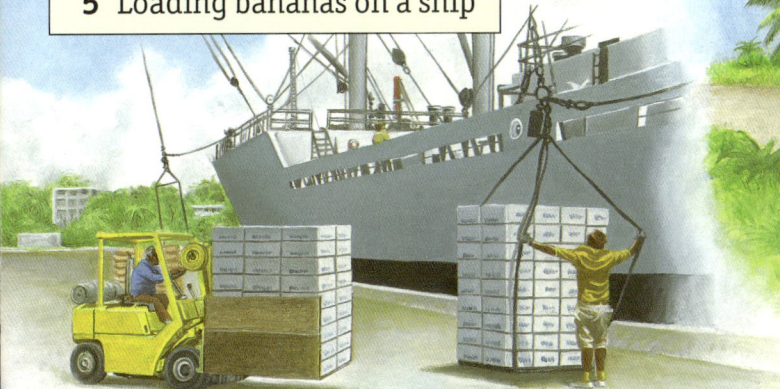

Things to do

Look at the pictures.

- Tell a story, in your own words, about how bananas are grown and sent abroad.

- How many different jobs can you find in the pictures?

- Which jobs are done by men and which by women?

6 Ship taking bananas to other countries

Made in St Lucia

Bananas cost a lot of money to produce. The St Lucians are getting less money for them now. The people in St Lucia know that they must find other jobs. It is not good for so many people to depend on one way of making a living.

The government wants more people to work in factories on the island. Factory buildings can be bought cheaply and the owners do not pay tax for 15 years.

In the past the only things made in St Lucia were soap, coconut oil, soft drinks, beer, cardboard boxes, clothes and furniture. These were sold to people on the island. Today, many more things are made in St Lucia such as sports clothes, electronics and toys. These things are sold to other countries. This is very important for St Lucia. It helps to provide more jobs, and more money for better roads and schools.

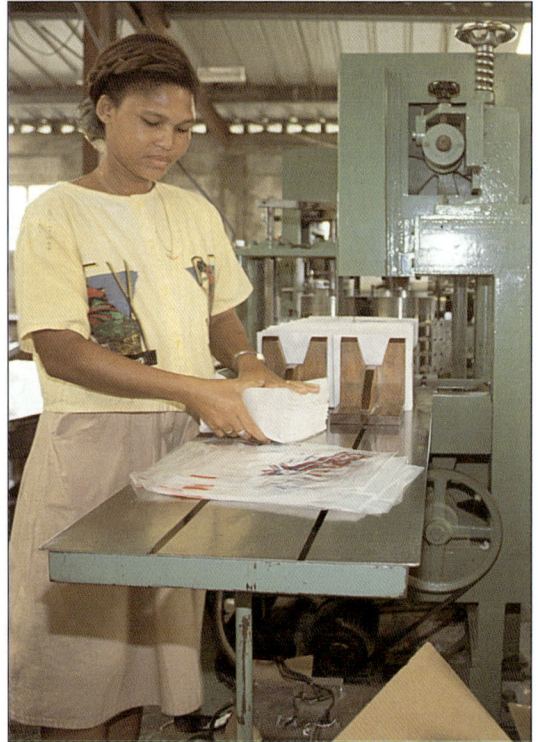

▲ This St Lucian woman works in a factory making kitchen rolls.

◀ A factory worker assembling electronic components.

◄ These huge vats are in the Windward and Leeward Brewery which makes drinks such as beer.

▼ This factory is the Windward and Leeward Brewery.

Wages in St Lucia

This is how much these people get paid for an hour's work. They get paid in Eastern Caribbean dollars.

Mechanic	5.15
Secretary	5.00
Truck driver	3.75
Carpenter	2.70
Factory worker	1.75

1 Eastern Caribbean dollar = 25p

Things to do

- Imagine you are trying to persuade a factory owner to set up a new factory in St Lucia. List the reasons why you think it is a good idea.

- Design a poster showing how the island is the perfect place for a factory.

Holiday island

The number of people who go to St Lucia for their holidays is growing. In 1964 there were only two hotels on the island with 20 rooms between them. There are now 40 hotels to choose from.

More people going on holiday to St Lucia means more jobs for St Lucians. Many of them have become taxi drivers or holiday guides. There are more jobs working in hotels and shops which sell goods for tourists. More people are needed to make the things for the tourists to buy.

There are many reasons why the island is popular:
- warm temperatures and lots of sun all year round
- beautiful beaches and coral reefs
- attractive scenery – rainforests and mountains
- historic places like Pigeon Point National Park
- wonderful nature reserves with rare animals and plants
- ideal for watersports like windsurfing and snorkelling
- interesting places to visit like volcanoes and waterfalls

It is still quite expensive to visit the Caribbean but it is getting cheaper. Many holiday companies now offer holidays on St Lucia and the other Caribbean islands.

Things to do

- Here is a list of different types of work. Copy the list and say if the number of jobs for each type of work is getting more or less.

    growing bananas
    taxi driving
    working in hotels
    factory work

- Do you think there might be any problems with the changes happening in St Lucia? Explain them.

Holidays in St Lucia

The St Lucian Hotel,
Reduit Beach

East Winds Inn,
The Bar-B-Q, Castries

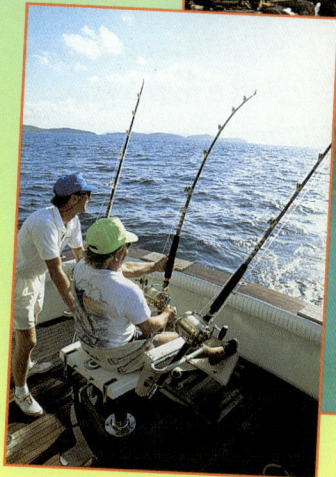

Sport fishing
from the
'Bobble Hatch'

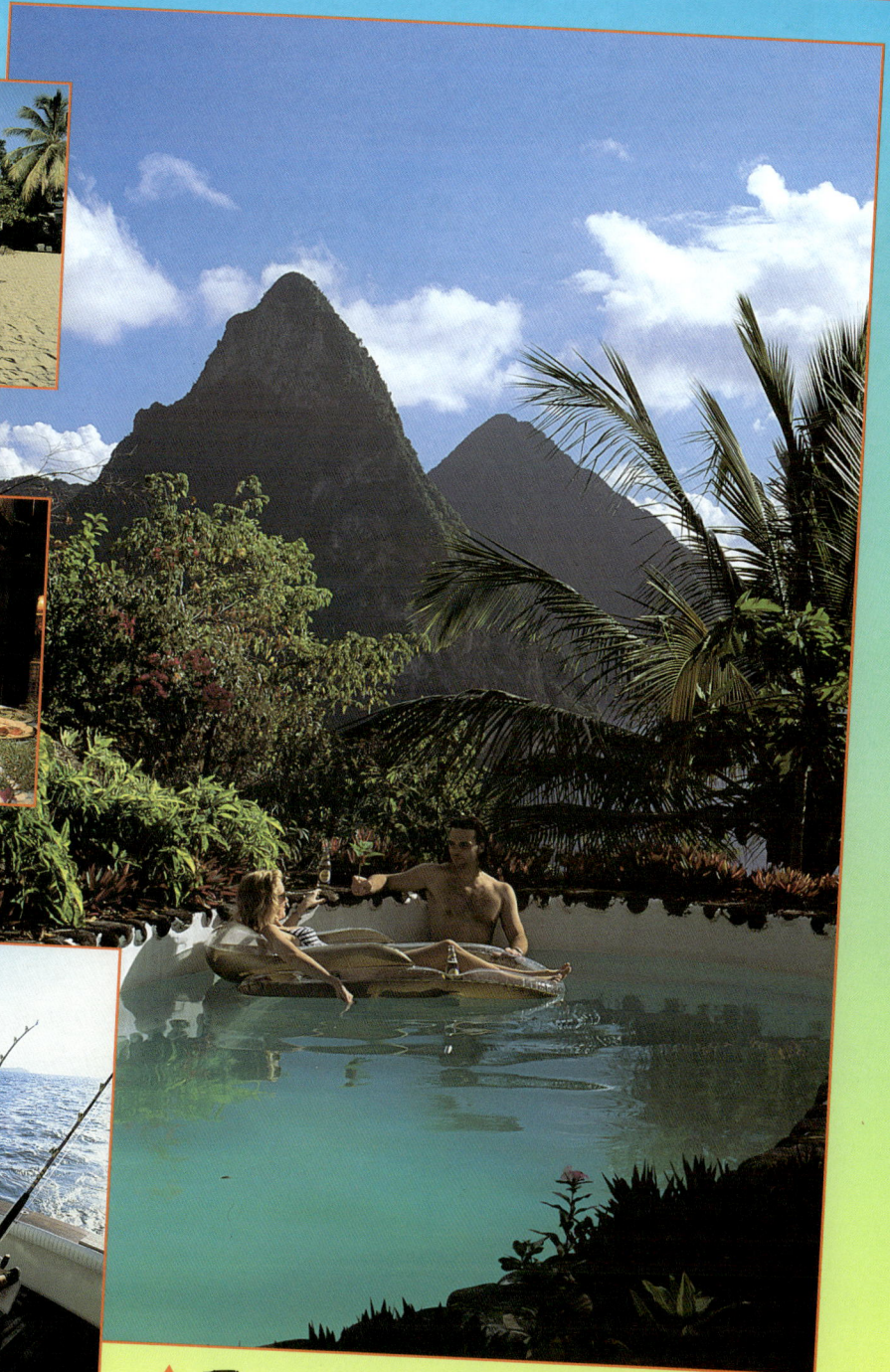

The pool at Cashew Villa Apartments

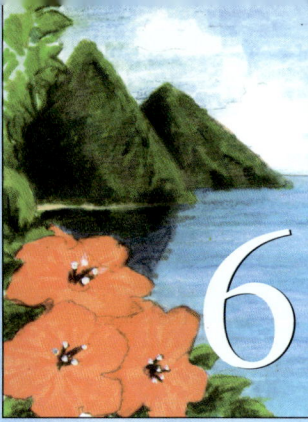

Wider world links

People and goods from St Lucia are found all over the world. There are many St Lucians living and working in Britain.

How is St Lucia linked to the rest of the world?

Fenna Monplaisir was born in St Lucia. She lives and works in Britain but she visits her family in St Lucia whenever she can. She travels by air because it is quick. There are flights from St Lucia to London, the USA, Canada and other parts of the world.

Fenna says: 'I left St Lucia because there is a wider choice of jobs in Britain. I miss the warm St Lucian weather and being able to spend so much time outdoors. The cities in Britain still seem huge to me compared to the towns and villages where I grew up.'

Think about

- Why did Fenna leave home?
- Why does she like going back to St Lucia?

Passenger liners bring hundreds of visitors to St Lucia each week. These huge ships are like floating hotels. They dock in Castries, sometimes staying only one day before sailing to another island.

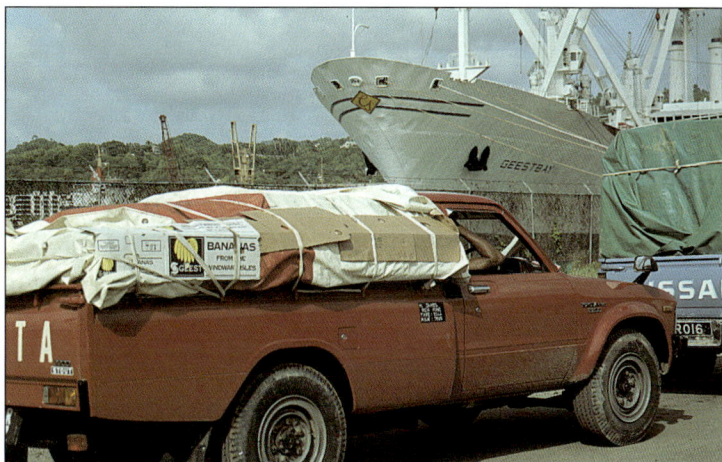

Think about

- Why are links between St Lucia and the rest of the world important for the future of the island?

- How many types of transport can you see on the plan below?

Goods are usually carried by sea. Cargo boats call at Castries and Vieux Fort. Most goods are carried in big metal boxes called containers.

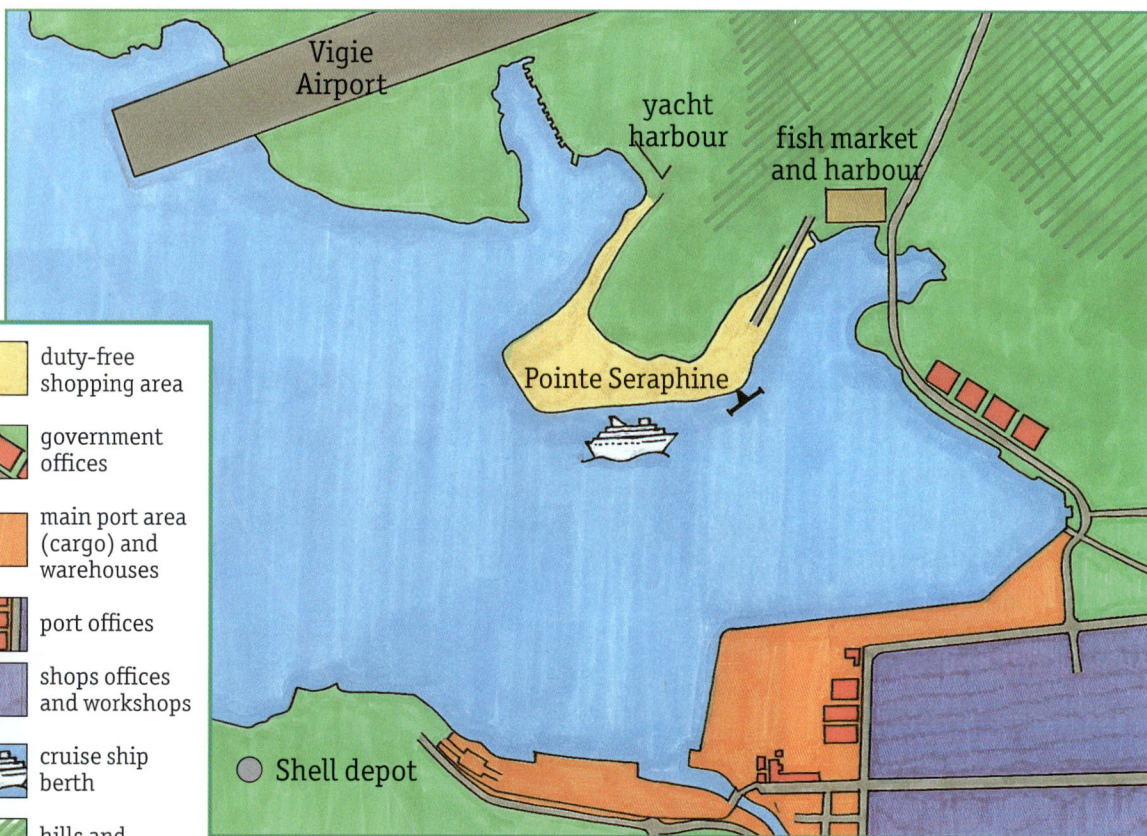

Legend:
- duty-free shopping area
- government offices
- main port area (cargo) and warehouses
- port offices
- shops offices and workshops
- cruise ship berth
- hills and houses

Vigie Airport

yacht harbour

fish market and harbour

Pointe Seraphine

○ Shell depot

▲ This is a plan of the harbour and waterfront in Castries.

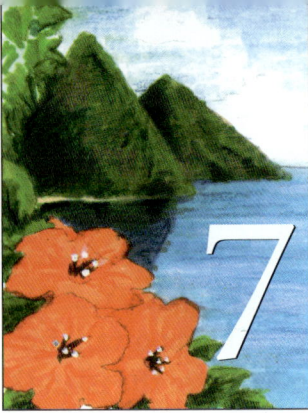

Changing land – changing lives

St Lucia is changing fast. New factories, shops and hotels are being built as well as modern houses. These changes mean new jobs to replace the work on banana farms. What the island will be like in the future depends on decisions being made today.

How is St Lucia changing?

At the weekends the Harveys like to visit relatives. Some of them live in the village of Choiseul. Mrs Harvey grew up in Choiseul and she notices many changes. Most houses now have water and electricity supplies and the fishermen have outboard motors on their canoes. Changes like this make life much easier for these people.

Think about

The Harveys sometimes wonder what changes will have taken place in ten years' time.

- What jobs do you think Gimel and Thia will be able to do?

St Lucia

Anse Ger

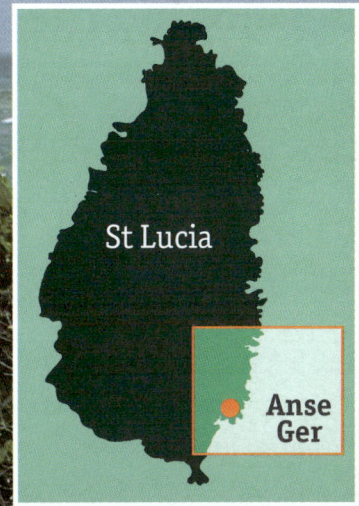

The land in this picture is near the village of Anse Ger. It is an area of trees and grassland where some cacti grow. There are mangrove swamps along the coast. Local people fish in the sea and collect fruits and other plants. Many have no jobs – some used to grow bananas and coconuts.

- How could St Lucians develop this area of land?

Developing the site

The land near Anse Ger may not stay as it is for long. Other parts of the island have been developed. Factories and hotels have been built in many similar places. A new hotel or factory could provide work but it might spoil the land and destroy the homes of many insects and birds.

▶ This is a factory site near Castries. Is there any land near you which is being built on?

▼ This new hotel is being built at Rodney Bay. What sort of jobs can people do in hotels and factories?

Whenever there are changes to the way in which land is used, people are affected in different ways. Here are four people who have different ideas about how to use the land at Anse Ger.

My neighbours and I grow bananas near Micoud but the work is hard and we do not make much money. We would like new jobs in a hotel or factory.

People enjoy the wildlife here. We should make another nature reserve. This will protect the land for the future.

This area is close to the international airport and nice beaches. Tourists would stay in a new hotel and spend their money in Micoud.

I could build a factory here quite cheaply. It is close to the airport and the sea port at Vieux Fort. There are good road links and people here need jobs.

Things to do

- Draw some pictures showing the different ways this land could be used.

- Under each picture list the good and the bad points about each of the four ideas.

- How would you use this land? Why would you make this choice?

St Lucia – the future

There are many changes happening in St Lucia. Like people everywhere, the Harvey children hope that their way of life will improve. St Lucians want new hospitals, schools and better roads. Tourism is growing and new factories are being built. This will mean more money for the island but it may lead to more problems.

What will St Lucia be like in the future?

You have learned about the climate and the landscape of St Lucia. This drawing shows how the 'natural system' of an island works. Many of the special things about St Lucia, like the scenery and the wildlife, depend on this natural system being cared for.

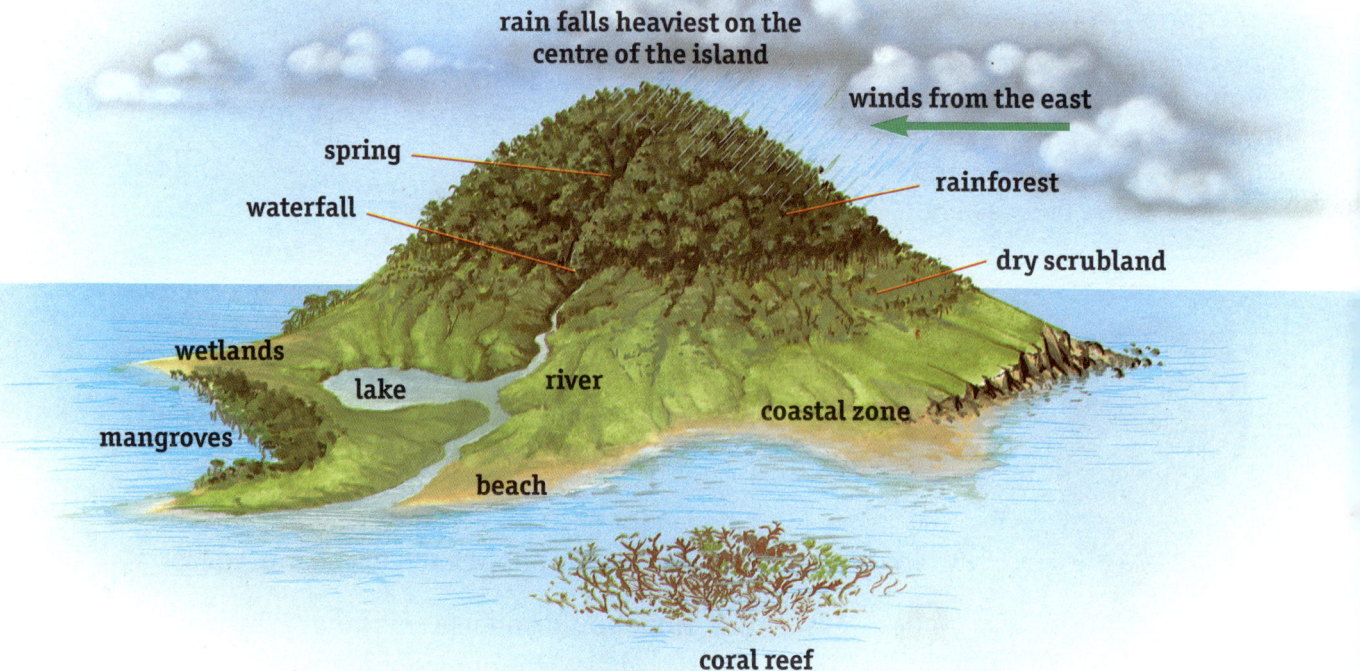

rain falls heaviest on the centre of the island

winds from the east

spring

waterfall

rainforest

dry scrubland

wetlands

lake

river

coastal zone

mangroves

beach

coral reef

Natural system

The diagram below shows what the island could look like if development is allowed to go ahead without control. Tourists are important to St Lucia, but too many hotels could damage the coastline. Trees are being cut down to make way for crops, new buildings and roads. However, forests are needed to protect the soil, to keep the air fresh and to store water.

Things to do

- Name some of the developments which might take place in St Lucia.

- Should St Lucia stay like the picture on page 44 or develop like the picture on this page?

- What are the good and bad points in each of these pictures?

- What would your ideal St Lucia be like in 2005?

Over-developed system

Conclusion

In this book you have found out about St Lucia – about the weather, about people and places, about the landscape and what it is like to live and work there. Some St Lucians have told you what they think about their island and what they hope for in the future. Look at the pictures and remember all you have found out about this question:

What is it like to live in St Lucia?

Things to do

- Draw some pictures showing what it is like in St Lucia. Remember to show:

  the weather

  people and places

  the landscape

  work and play

- For each picture of St Lucia, draw another one to show what it is like where you live.

- Under each pair of pictures say what is the same and what is different, like this:

  In St Lucia the weather is…

  Where I live the weather is…

- Now make a display for your classroom about what life is like in St Lucia.

St Lucia is a small island in the Caribbean Sea. It is hot all year round and it often rains. The rain is very heavy but it soon dries in the bright sunshine. There are mountains on the island. They were made by volcanoes. It is a very green and beautiful place.

Nearly half of the people in St Lucia live in the capital city, Castries. It is by far the biggest town on the island. Castries is also a port. It has the most sheltered harbour in the Caribbean.

The number of people who go to St Lucia for their holidays is growing. In 1964 there were only 2 hotels on the island with 20 rooms between them. There are now 40 hotels to choose from.

There are many different jobs in St Lucia: growing bananas, fishing, making things in factories, cooking for tourists in hotels and many more. People have been doing some of these jobs for thousands of years. Some jobs, like those to do with holidays, are quite new.

Index